Save Energy, Save Earth

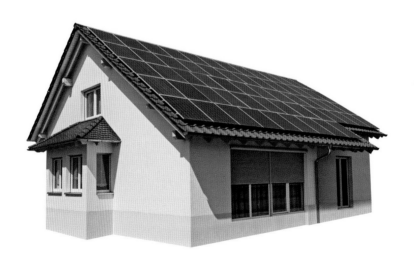

THIS EDITION
Editorial Management by Oriel Square
Produced for DK by WonderLab Group LLC
Jennifer Emmett, Erica Green, Kate Hale, *Founders*

Editors Grace Hill Smith, Libby Romero, Maya Myers, Michaela Weglinski;
Photography Editors Kelley Miller, Annette Kiesow, Nicole DiMella; **Managing Editor** Rachel Houghton;
Designers Project Design Company; **Researcher** Michelle Harris; **Copy Editor** Lori Merritt;
Indexer Connie Binder; **Proofreader** Larry Shea; **Reading Specialist** Dr. Jennifer Albro;
Curriculum Specialist Elaine Larson

Published in the United States by DK Publishing
1745 Broadway, 20th Floor, New York, NY 10019

Copyright © 2023 Dorling Kindersley Limited
DK, a Division of Penguin Random House LLC
23 24 25 26 10 9 8 7 6 5 4 3 2 1
001-334111-July/2023

A catalog record for this book
is available from the Library of Congress.
HC ISBN: 978-0-7440-7521-2
PB ISBN: 978-0-7440-7522-9

DK books are available at special discounts when purchased in bulk for sales promotions, premiums,
fundraising, or educational use. For details, contact: DK Publishing Special Markets,
1745 Broadway, 20th Floor, New York, NY 10019
SpecialSales@dk.com

Printed and bound in China

The publisher would like to thank the following for their kind permission to reproduce their images:
a=above; c=center; b=below; l=left; r=right; t=top; b/g=background

123RF.com: epicstockmedia 36tl, martinkay78 20-21b, nerthuz 20tl, Prasit Rodphan 41l, Patrik Slezak 16tl;
Alamy Stock Photo: Reuters / Philippe Wojazer 38tl; **Depositphotos Inc:** atitayapimpa1234@gmail.com 42cl, serezniy 10tl;
Dorling Kindersley: Clive Streeter / The Science Museum, London 6tl; **Dreamstime.com:** Africa Rising Agency 34b,
Andrey Armyagov 37tr, Aliaksandr Baiduk 19tr, Milos Bogicevic 24tl, Pichit Boonhuad 44tl, Brzozowsskipawell 40tl, Btwcapture 30br,
Charlieb34 16-17b, Chernetskaya 26tl, Derektenhue 33tr, Dvmsimages 21tr, Korneev Evgeny 25crb, Fotorutkowscy 35t, Filip Fuxa 14tl,
Haiyin 42tr, Anthony Heflin 7bl, Ilfede 27tr, Ankit Jangir 25tr, Jezper 4-5, Ferli Achirulli Kamaruddin 18-19b, James Kirkikis 7tr,
Klingsup 9b, KPixMining 29tr, Octavian Lazar 18tl, Ljupco 41tr, Luchschen 38-39b, Maldives001 28-29t, Dimitar Marinov / Oorka 14cl,
32-33, Aliaksandr Mazurkevich 26-27b, Alexandr Mitiuc 36-37b, Monkey Business Images 45tr, Msg-s 43tr, Nataliia Mysak 8tl,
Sergey Novikov 13br, Oxfordsquare 1b, Sean Pavone 10-11, Photka 28cla, Photopips 30tl, Svetlana Popova 13tr, Manuel Ribeiro 22tl,
Bryan Roschetzky 23bl, Francesco Scatena 31tr, Scharfsinn86 39tr, Secretside 17tc, Selitbul 15b, Joa Souza 43bl, Starast 3cb,
Prarinya Thonghyad 8br, Usataro 13bl, Dmytro Zinkevych 44-45b; **Getty Images:** Irina Gundareva / 500px 29crb, Bettmann 12br,
Joe Raedle / Staff 38cl; **Getty Images / iStock:** E+ / EXTREME-PHOTOGRAPHER 24-25b, Thomas Faull 6bl,
Daniel Lozano Gonzalez 12tl, Photos.com 9tr

Cover images: *Front:* **Dreamstime.com:** Visdia

All other images © Dorling Kindersley
For more information see: www.dkimages.com

For the curious
www.dk.com

Level
4

Save Energy, Save Earth

Jen Szymanski

CONTENTS

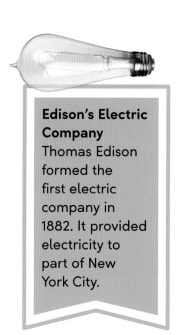

EVERYDAY ENERGY

Getting up in the morning can be pretty tough. You drag yourself out of bed, flip on the lights, and jump in the shower. Then, you eat a quick breakfast, maybe pack a lunch, and rush off to school. Have you ever stopped to think about how easy it is to do these things?

In the past, lots of kids had chores to do in the morning. Before the sun rose, they gathered wood and carried buckets of water back from the well. They needed wood to start a fire. Fire provided heat and light. Without fire, people couldn't cook breakfast or warm the chilly water so they could bathe.

The kids did these chores as quickly as they could, for they often had a long walk to school. If they were late, they wouldn't get a seat by the schoolhouse stove. The stove kept them warm, and light from its fire made it a lot easier to read.

Energy, like heat and electricity, is a lot easier to tap into today. Aren't you glad?

Getting Connected
In 1925, only half of the homes in the United States were connected to electric power. Today, almost every home in the US has access to electricity.

Horsepower
The first school bus was used in 1827. It was pulled by horses and could carry 25 children.

Calories
Food labels use the term "calories" to describe how much energy is found in the food you eat. Your body changes the energy in food into a form that it can use.

Energy is a basic human need. People use it to build homes and to keep their homes warm or cool. Ovens use energy to cook food. Refrigerators use energy to keep food cold so it doesn't spoil quickly. Energy lights up the night, gets travelers to school and work, and helps keep our lives safe and comfortable.

Most people take it for granted. But what is energy? Scientists define energy as the ability to do work or the ability to make something move or change.

The Study of Energy
A physicist is a scientist who studies energy.

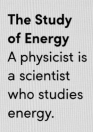

There are many kinds of energy. And absolutely nothing in the entire universe would happen if it weren't for some form of energy.

Right now, your body is using chemical and electrical energy to keep your heart beating. You used the energy of motion when you picked up this book. And a special kind of electric energy is speeding through your brain as you make sense of the words you read.

A New Term
In the early 1800s, scientist Thomas Young became the first person credited with using the term "energy."

Calculating Costs
It only costs a few dollars per year to charge a computer tablet.

Energy makes things work. Wind sends sailboats skimming across the water. Gasoline makes many cars and trucks move. Electricity powers computers and other devices. The list goes on and on!

Energy Factors
Geographic location and climate affect how much energy a household uses. The type of home, how many people live there, and how much energy those people use are also important factors.

Our society has an enormous need for energy. Factories use energy to manufacture everything from clothing to computers. Other industries use energy to process and package food and to deliver it to markets. It takes energy to pump water from a source, to treat it so it's safe to drink, and to move it to homes and businesses. Energy helps us communicate by computer, phone, and even postal mail.

Energy connects people, whether they're in the same room, in a different part of town, or in another country. It holds our civilization together!

Increasing Need
The number of people on Earth continues to grow. More people means that we will need more energy in the future than we do now.

SOURCES OF ENERGY

Meeting the world's growing need for energy wouldn't be a problem if we could just make more energy. But we can't—energy can neither be created nor destroyed.

A law in science is something that has been shown over and over again to be true. Physicist Albert Einstein was famous for studying a scientific law that states "energy is neither created nor destroyed. It can only be changed from one form to another."

Albert Einstein studied energy.

Light Energy to Heat
You can feel energy changing forms if you wear a dark-colored shirt on a hot, sunny day. The dark color absorbs the Sun's light energy and changes it to heat.

When people talk about making energy, it doesn't mean that energy is being created from nothing. Making energy means taking a form of energy stored in a source and changing it into a form that we want to use.

Often, that form of energy is electricity. Most electricity is made, or generated, when energy stored in a source is changed into heat and used to produce steam. The steam is used to turn the blades of a machine called a turbine. Spinning turbines are connected to generators that make electricity.

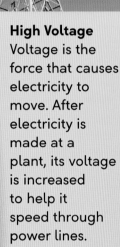

High Voltage
Voltage is the force that causes electricity to move. After electricity is made at a plant, its voltage is increased to help it speed through power lines.

These giant turbines create electricity inside the power plant at the Hoover Dam. The dam lies on the Colorado River, along the border of Nevada and Arizona in the USA.

Energy of Motion
Energy of motion is called kinetic energy.

Geothermal Champion
Iceland is a leader in geothermal energy. Its six plants generate about 25 percent of the country's power.

A Different Kind of Farm
Large groups of windmills are called wind farms. Wind farms are built in areas where the wind blows steadily.

Almost all of the energy on Earth starts in one place: the Sun. The Sun's solar energy won't run out for billions of years, So, it is considered to be a renewable resource. Renewable resources can be used over and over again.

On Earth, sunlight's energy is often captured by plants. Plants change energy from the Sun into chemical energy in the form of sugar. When an animal eats a plant, the energy moves from the plant into the animal. If that animal is eaten, the energy moves on to the animal that ate it.

There are plenty of other renewable resources on Earth. Wood that comes from trees can be replaced in a relatively short period of time. Wind and water are also sources of renewable energy. So is heat energy that comes from below Earth's surface. It's called geothermal energy.

There are challenges to using renewable sources of energy. They may be limitless in supply, but they are not found everywhere. Power plants that make electricity using geothermal energy, for example, can only be built in locations where there is a lot of heat right below Earth's surface.

This geothermal power plant in Krafla, Iceland, has been in operation since 1977.

Mighty Water
Hydropower is energy generated by the force of moving water. People have used hydropower for thousands of years.

Long Life
Some nuclear wastes stay radioactive for a thousand years or more.

Fracking
Fracking is a process in which people squirt a fluid containing water, sand, and chemicals into the ground at a high pressure. This cracks open rocks so trapped nonrenewable resources can be pumped out. Scientists worry that the fluid can pollute groundwater.

At the moment, people use nonrenewable resources to meet most of their needs. Fossil fuels—like coal, oil, and natural gas—are the most commonly used. They formed over millions of years as heat and pressure acted upon the trapped remains of ancient plants and animals in Earth's crust.

Uranium is a metal element. It is a nonrenewable resource that is used to make nuclear energy. As the particles in uranium are split apart, they release a lot of heat that makes steam. The steam spins the turbine that drives a generator, producing electricity. Unlike some other metals, uranium cannot be manufactured. Once it's gone, it's gone.

In some parts of the world, people get almost three-quarters of their energy from fossil fuels. But there are many downsides to relying on nonrenewable resources to meet energy needs.

Mining coal and uranium and drilling for oil and natural gas harms ecosystems. Burning fossil fuels releases greenhouse gases and particle pollution that contribute to climate change. Uranium is radioactive. It can cause health problems, such as cancer in people and animals. In addition, nonrenewable resources aren't being replaced. These energy sources will eventually run out.

Acid Precipitation
Burning fossil fuels releases harmful chemicals into the air. The chemicals mix with water in the atmosphere to form a weak acid. The acid falls back to Earth as acid rain or snow, which eats away at buildings and hurts living things.

Some scientists predict that fossil fuels will run out in about a hundred years.

Vampire Devices
Vampire devices, such as televisions, suck power any time they're plugged in—even if they're turned off. This can increase a monthly electric bill by at least 10 percent.

Minimizing Waste
More than 60 percent of the energy made in some power plants is lost as heat. The power plants try to capture that heat and use it to make electricity so that only 20 to 40 percent of total energy is wasted.

WASTING ENERGY

Energy can't be destroyed, but it can definitely be wasted. Energy is wasted when it's not used to do work.

Believe it or not, a lot of energy is wasted in power plants! When fossil fuels are burned in power plants, they create heat, which creates steam that is used to make electricity. But not all of the heat energy generated in a power plant ends up making steam. Some is wasted when it is lost to the air. Then, when the electricity travels away from power plants through wires, some of it changes back into heat. So, even more energy is lost.

People waste all kinds of energy at home, too. They forget to turn lights off when they leave a room. They stand with the refrigerator door open for a long time while deciding what to have for a snack. They sit in a long drive-thru line at a fast-food restaurant without moving. This wastes energy in gasoline.

Even when people try to conserve power, they may be wasting energy. Some devices even use energy when their power switch is off.

Home Energy Wasters
Three of the biggest energy wasters in a home are running the dishwasher half full, washing all laundry in hot water, and setting the thermostat up too high in the winter or too low in the summer.

Going Electric
Some cars don't have a gas tank. Instead, they have a battery and run completely on electricity. These vehicles don't release pollutants when they run, so they are good for the environment.

Out the Window
Windows are a big reason why home energy costs are so high. Heat that either goes out or comes in windows accounts for up to 30 percent of a home's energy bill.

Another way people waste energy is to use more energy than they need to do work.

Efficiency is a way to measure how much energy is used to do something. If something is not efficient, it uses more energy than is needed. Turning up the thermostat in the winter and having all the windows open at the same time isn't an efficient way to keep a house warm. People can use a lot less energy if they keep the windows closed so heat can't escape.

Fuel efficiency is used to describe how much gasoline a car uses to go a certain distance. It's often stated in miles per gallon or kilometers per liter.

Gas-guzzling sport utility vehicles (SUVs) and larger pickup trucks aren't very fuel efficient. They have their uses, but many of these larger vehicles only get about 20 miles for every gallon of gas (8.5 km per liter). Smaller, more fuel-efficient cars can get 30 miles to the gallon (12.8 km per liter) or even more.

Early Fuel Efficiency
Some of the first cars ever built were more fuel efficient than today's big trucks and SUVs. The Ford Model T got as much as 21 miles per gallon (8.9 km per liter).

Fuel Savers
Hybrid cars have a gasoline-powered engine and a motor that runs on electricity. The electric motor does some of the work, so these cars use less gas than other cars do. Some hybrid cars get about 50 miles to the gallon (21.3 km per liter)!

Mine Runoff
Even coal mines that aren't active cause pollution. Mining coal leaves behind rocks that contain sulfur. When these come into contact with water from rain or snow, they form sulfuric acid, which pollutes streams and rivers.

Using more fuel-efficient cars and trying not to waste energy are both good ways to save Earth's limited supply of fossil fuels. And the less of those we use, the better.

That's because using fossil fuels are causing Earth's climate to change. Earth's average temperature is going up, sea levels are rising, and major weather events are becoming more severe.

Why is this happening? The energy stored in coal, gas, and oil contains a large amount of carbon. When fossil fuels are burned, the carbon in them is released into Earth's atmosphere as carbon dioxide (CO_2.) Carbon dioxide is one of the greenhouse gases that causes global warming.

Climate change causes increased flooding because a warmer atmosphere holds and releases more water.

The upswing in CO_2 began during the Industrial Revolution, which occurred between 1760 and 1840. Hundreds of new factories were built all over the world, many of which used fossil fuels to generate energy.

Since then, people have continued to use more and more fossil fuels. The amount of CO_2 in Earth's atmosphere is higher now than it has ever been in recent history.

Greenhouse Effect
Gases such as carbon dioxide act like a blanket in the atmosphere, trapping the Sun's heat next to Earth's surface. It's a little like how glass traps the Sun's heat inside a greenhouse, which is why scientists nicknamed what happens the "greenhouse effect."

Sleep Saves Energy
Devices that go into "sleep mode" use less power than those that are on all of the time.

SAVING ENERGY

People can help reverse this trend by conserving, or saving, energy. And fortunately, there are so many different ways to do it.

It all begins with the three R's: reduce, reuse, and recycle. The three R's are more than an easy phrase to remember—they're a list of things that work to help save energy.

Reducing, or decreasing, the amount of energy we use comes down to making smart choices.

For example, people have many different appliances in their homes, such as dishwashers, washing machines, and furnaces. Different models of appliances use different amounts of energy. Newer appliances often are much more efficient than older ones. Buying more efficient appliances is one way that people can choose to reduce the amount of energy they use.

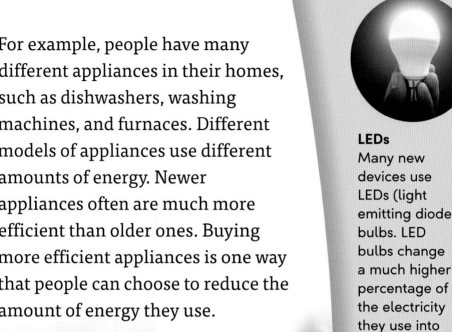

LEDs
Many new devices use LEDs (light emitting diodes) bulbs. LED bulbs change a much higher percentage of the electricity they use into light than other bulbs do.

Better Bulbs
Only about 10 percent of the electric energy in traditional light bulbs is turned into light. The other 90 percent is changed to heat and is lost.

Reconsider Plastic Bottles
Over half a trillion plastic bottles were made and sold in 2021. The energy used to make them could be saved if people chose to use refillable water bottles instead.

Another way to reduce waste is to buy fewer new things to begin with. Factories use enormous amounts of energy to manufacture goods. It also takes a lot of energy to move things on airplanes, ships, trains, and trucks from factories to stores.

People can choose to wait to buy a new version of an electronic device. They can choose to wear clothes longer instead of going shopping for something new. These choices mean less energy is consumed in making new items.

Reusing things instead of buying new things saves energy, too. Buy used clothing at a thrift shop. Drink from a refillable water bottle. Donate used items so someone else can reuse them and keep the cycle going. Each of these choices means new things won't have to be made.

One simple action might not seem like much, but everything adds up. Many people taking small steps can make a big difference.

Transportation Options
Companies can reduce how much energy they use by choosing efficient ways to transport goods. Large ships use the least amount of fuel. They may be twice as fuel efficient as planes and up to 20 times more efficient than trucks.

Single Stream
Know the rules. Some recycling centers require people to separate different types of materials into different bins. Others allow people to put all kinds of materials in the same bin.

Of course, people do need to buy new things sometimes. And sometimes the things people need can't be reused. The good news is that many products used in homes and schools can be recycled, including paper, glass, metal, and plastics.

It takes less energy to make something from recycled materials than from new raw materials. For example, it takes about 95 percent less energy to make a can from recycled metal than from scratch.

Very little of the plastic produced is successfully recycled. It takes hundreds of years for plastic items to decompose in landfills.

Recycled materials can be used to make some pretty surprising things. Plastic yogurt cups and bags can become park benches. Old clothes can be woven into carpets. Even the soles of running shoes can be recycled and used to make sidewalks and basketball courts.

As a bonus, recycling also keeps trash out of landfills. Overflowing landfills can pollute ecosystems, which then need even more energy to clean up.

eWaste
Things like dead batteries and old cell phones are called "eWaste." These items contain metals and other materials that are harmful to people's health. They must be recycled in a special way.

Save the Trees
Recycling paper works. Every 2,000 pounds (907 kg) of paper recycled can save more than 15 trees, hundreds of gallons of fossil fuels, and thousands of gallons of water.

Recycling Triangle
To identify recycling bins, just look for the recycling symbol. It is a triangle made of three arrows: one for reduce, one for reuse, and one for recycle.

Decomposers
Composting is possible thanks to the help of decomposers like worms, insects, and mushrooms. These and other living things break down dead plant and animal matter, which helps nutrients get back into the soil.

To tackle most types of recycling, you need the help of recycling centers. All you have to do is make sure that recyclable materials stay out of the trash, get cleaned, and make it into the correct recycling bin.

But there are types of recycling people can do at home, too. Compost is a good example. Compost is decaying or rotting material that can be used to help plants grow. Leaves, grass clippings, and even some vegetable and fruit scraps from the kitchen can be made into compost. When the compost is ready, you can use it to grow new fruits and vegetables that you can eat.

You can also turn something old into something new. An empty plastic jar might make a good flowerpot. A juice carton can be turned into a simple birdfeeder, or broken crayons might be made into a candle. There's practically no limit to what can be recycled with a little creativity.

Upcycling
Sometimes, goods made from recycled materials are better or more valuable than the original material they came from. This is called upcycling. Examples include tote bags made from old billboards and sweaters spun from yarn made from empty two-liter plastic bottles.

Up to Code
One way to save energy is to construct new homes and buildings in ways that make them energy efficient. Many areas have rules called codes to make sure this happens.

Following the three R's helps people conserve energy. But conservation isn't enough. Sustainability is the key to the future.

Using energy resources sustainably means meeting our own energy needs while making sure that there's enough for the future. Despite the many renewable sources of energy available, people still rely heavily on nonrenewable resources to meet their needs. This is not sustainable.

One of the biggest problems we face in saving energy is ourselves. It takes time, money, and effort to try new methods of generating energy. Often, it's just easier and cheaper to keep doing what we've been doing than to try and solve the world's energy problems.

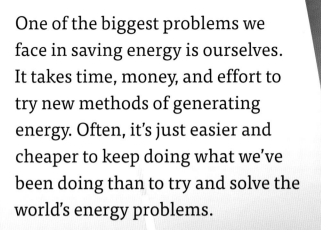

Sunny Money
Some power companies buy extra electricity from customers that have installed solar panels on their property.

Energy from Light
Solar cells change the Sun's energy directly into electricity by releasing tiny particles called electrons. The electrons are channeled into a wire that connects to a power station or a battery.

FUTURE TECHNOLOGIES

Creativity is the key to solving Earth's energy problems. Would you ride in a bus that runs on vegetable oil? Or take a flight on a plane fueled by pond scum? Someday you might! Scientists and engineers are looking at lots of interesting ways to make sure the world has enough energy both now and in the future.

Biomass is plant material that can be used to make biofuels. Biofuels can be used alone to power vehicles or mixed with regular gasoline to make the gas last longer. Some biofuels, such as ethanol and biodiesel, have been widely used for many years.

At the Pump
Ethanol and biodiesel are common biofuels. Most ethanol comes from corn. Biodiesel is made from sources like cooking oil and animal fat.

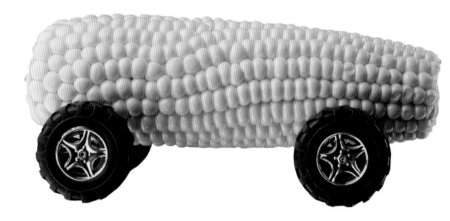

Other biofuels aren't as commonly used—at least not yet. Ocean oil spills spell disaster for plants and animals in marine ecosystems. But what if the spilled fuel were made from algae? There would be far less damage.

Algae is a good source for biofuel. It can be harvested from the ocean or grown in tanks on land. However, the process used to make this kind of biofuel is expensive. Scientists are searching for ways to improve the process so that algae might be a common biofuel choice someday.

Better Fires
For thousands of years, people have cut down trees to create fires for heat and cooking. Modern stoves burn wood chippings, grass, and straw instead. This conserves fossil fuels and saves trees.

Wave Power
If waves are ever used as an energy source, scientists think they could supply over half of the energy needs along the coasts of the United States.

Oceans can be a valuable source of power, too. Oceans are always moving. Waves crash into the shore. Tides flow in and out. Ocean currents flow thousands of miles. Can this movement be used to generate electricity? In some places, it already is.

Tides rise and fall twice every day. Some dams take advantage of this predictable pattern. They trap the water in a bay at high tide. When the tide goes out, they release the water behind the dam. The water flows to meet the ocean level at low tide. This force is used to turn turbines and generate electricity.

Many scientists think strong ocean currents could spin a turbine's blades, too. But this technology isn't quite ready to use yet. The ocean's saltwater corrodes the machines needed to make power.

Scientists also worry about how the equipment might add stress to already fragile ocean ecosystems. Building the machines needed to tap into the power of ocean currents could destroy marine habitats. Someday, though, this technology might be perfected and homes could be powered by the ocean.

Instant A/C
Ocean water can get quite chilly. Someday, ocean water might be pumped through special systems in buildings to cool them down. A system like this would use less energy than an all-electric air conditioner.

Air Car
A few companies have made tiny cars that run on compressed air. Enough energy is created by air escaping from a tank to set the engine—and the car—in motion.

Blast Off!
Liquid hydrogen provided the power to send Artemis 1 into space. Artemis 1 is the first step toward sending astronauts to Mars.

Hydrogen could be another source of fuel. Hydrogen is an element. An element is a substance that cannot be broken down into simpler substances. Hydrogen is one of the most common elements. It's found in air and water and is part of all living things.

Hydrogen burns well—really well. It burns with so much energy that it's part of the fuel that launches rockets into space. But there's a major problem with using hydrogen fuel in other places. Hydrogen can catch fire quickly, so it's hard to use safely.

Hydrogen fuel cells, though, are a different story. These fuel cells, which may someday power cars, are safe. One benefit of using hydrogen fuel cells is that they are clean energy. They don't release any carbon dioxide. The only things that come from the exhaust pipes of these cars are warm air and water vapor.

When hydrogen reacts with oxygen, it generates electricity that powers electric motors. Researchers are finding new ways to use hydrogen as an alternative fuel.

Poop Power
When solids—or poop—are digested at a wastewater treatment plant, they produce methane gas. In some places, this biogas is collected, cleaned, and used as fuel for cars and trucks.

Layer Up or Down

Over half of the energy used in the average home is used for heating and cooling. Rather than moving the thermostat up or down a few degrees, put on or take off a sweatshirt. This can save both energy and money.

HOW YOU CAN HELP

People have a huge challenge ahead of them. Having enough energy to meet everyone's needs is a problem that affects every human being on Earth. And every person will play a role in finding the solution. No matter your age, there are things you can do to help, both now and in the future.

The easiest thing you can do is find ways to save energy. And the simplest way is to change your habits. Turn off lights when you leave a room. If you see lights on in an empty room, turn them off, too.

Saving energy doesn't have to be a chore. Turn it into a game with friends. Plan a scavenger hunt where you explore the house searching for plugged-in devices. When you see something plugged in that nobody is using, check with an adult to see if it's okay to unplug it. If so, do it! Small actions can add up to big energy savings later on.

Save While Snacking

Do you take your time scouring the fridge for your favorite snack? Don't! If you choose snacks quickly, you could save enough energy each year to run a washing machine 50 times!

Tap into Water
Turning off the tap when you brush your teeth in the morning and at night saves four to eight gallons (15 to 30 liters) of water a day. That's about 200 gallons (757 liters) of water a month!

There are many kinds of energy, and you can help conserve each one. Even people who don't drive can help the world use less gasoline. Making fewer shopping trips—in your own car or a cab—helps save fuel. To limit trips, make a list and check it twice. This saves both fuel and time!

When you must go somewhere, think about how you're traveling. Can you get a ride with someone else going to the same place? Can you take a bus? Can you walk or ride a bike? Each time you use a more energy-efficient travel option, you save fuel.

It takes energy to move water from one place to another. It takes energy to make water safe to drink. To save energy and water, make wiser choices. Take shorter showers. Fill up the sink to rinse dishes instead of rinsing them under running water.

Planting a tree in the right spot can save energy, too. Trees create shade so it takes less energy to keep homes cool.

Shower vs. Tub
It takes 10 to 25 gallons (38 to 95 liters) of water to take a shower. It takes up to 70 gallons (265 liters) of water to fill a tub.

Tips for Planting Trees
To save the most energy, plant trees on the east and west sides of a house. These sides of a house receive 50 percent more sunlight than the north and south sides do.

Green Jobs
Careers in the clean energy field are sometimes called "green" jobs because they're helpful to the environment.

Earth's energy problems will not go away, and solving them won't be easy. But scientists and engineers are trying.

Scientists of all kinds, including those that study Earth and the environment, are searching for new ways to use the energy that's all around us. Could our body heat be used to power up a mobile phone? Maybe the energy from feet pounding on a dance floor could produce enough electricity to light up a building. Scientists ask questions, and then they do experiments to try and find answers.

Engineers invent and design new technologies to solve problems. Sometimes, it's a new twist on an old idea, such as an air conditioner that uses less electricity. Sometimes, it's something brand-new, such as a soccer ball that collects energy each time it's kicked. Engineers also invent new or more efficient processes that give people different ways to use energy from a resource.

Are you interested in science or engineering? Maybe someday you will discover a solution to Earth's energy challenges. Until then, learn all you can ... and do your part to save energy!

Bright Future Experts who study careers suggest that jobs in the field of energy will continue to grow.

GLOSSARY

Acid precipitation
Precipitation like rain or snow that has mixed with chemicals in the air and become acidic

Biomass
Plant material that can be used to make fuel

Calorie
A unit for measuring the amount of energy in food

Conserve
To save or to make sure there is enough of something for later use

Efficiency
A measure of how much work is done by a certain amount of energy

Energy
The ability to do work or the ability to make something move or change

Generator
A machine that makes electricity

Geothermal
Heat produced inside Earth

Hydropower
Power generated by the movement of water

Kinetic energy
The energy of motion

Nonrenewable
Something that cannot be replaced

Renewable
Something that either never runs out or can be replaced quickly

Sustainability
A measure of how well a product or process meets the needs of people both now and in the future

Turbine
A machine connected to a generator that spins

Voltage
The force that causes electricity to move

INDEX

QUIZ

Answer the questions to see what you have learned. Check your answers in the key below.

1. What is energy?

2. True or False: Scientists can create energy.

3. What natural resource is used to make hydropower?

4. What do coal, oil, and natural gas have in common?

5. What word is used to describe how much work is done by a certain amount of energy?

6. What are the "three R's?"

7. What is biofuel made from?

8. True or False: People use oceans as an energy source.

1. The ability to do work 2. False 3. Moving water
4. They are nonrenewable sources of energy 5. Efficiency
6. Reduce, reuse, recycle 7. Plants or other biomass 8. True